UNKNOWN AUTHOR

Be a Slug

Ben Ford

"Youth has no age..."
Pablo Picasso

FIRST STEP! GET YOURSELF NAKED. THAT'S RIGHT. YOU HAVE TO BE FULLY NUDE TO PERFORM THIS ACT! TAKE OFF YOUR SHIRT, BLOUSE, PANTS, SKIRT, DRESS AND ESPECIALLY SOCKS. OH, MAN, HOW CAN YOU PRETEND TO BE A SLUG AND HAVE SOCKS ON. DON'T BE AN UNCULTURED SWINE AND TAKE YOUR SOCKS OFF. IF YOU ARE A WOMAN, YOU MAY KEEP YOUR PANTIES, BUT IT IS NOT NECESSARY.

CORRECTION!!!

IF YOU DO HAVE A SPECIAL SLUG SUIT, THEN IGNORE THE FIRST STEP. (DON'T ASK ME WHERE YOU CAN FIND IT, SEARCH THE INTERNET CAREFULLY.)

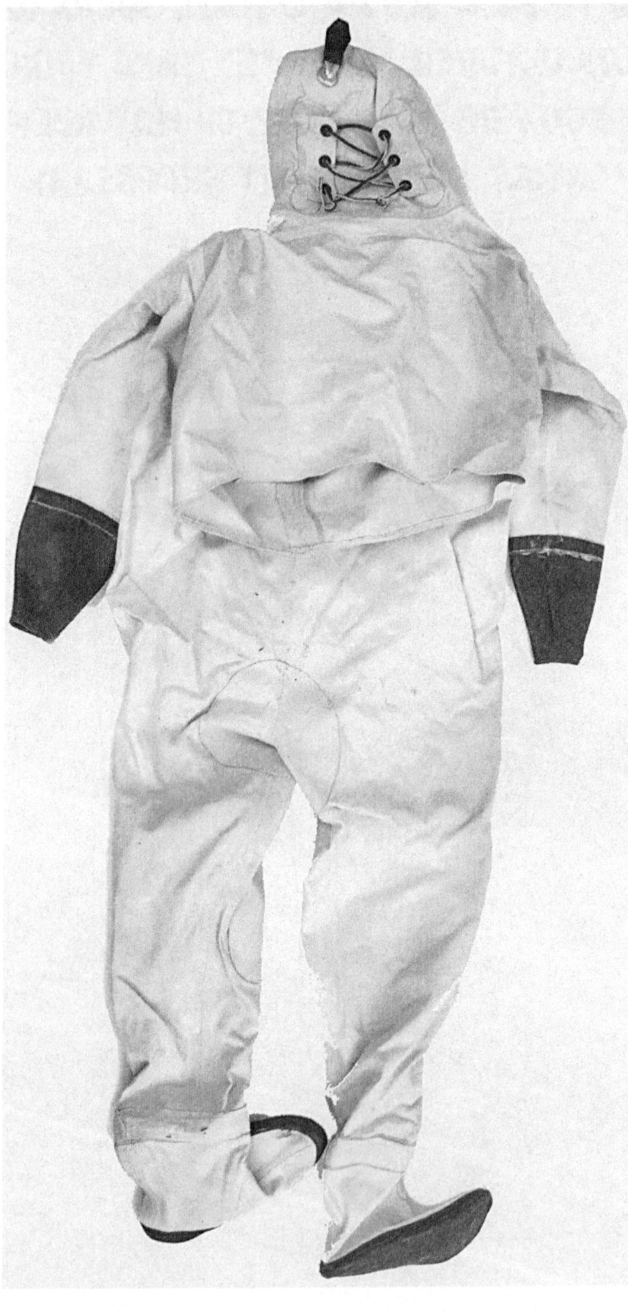

NEXT STEP IS THE OOZE OF YOUR CHOOSING. MOST PEOPLE USE VASELINE OR HONEY, BOTH ARE GOOD AND EASILY WASHABLE...I THINK.

REGARDLESS OF YOUR CHOICE, DON'T EVER, EVER, E-V-E-R IN YOUR LIFE USE GLUE! I LEARNED THIS A HARD WAY.

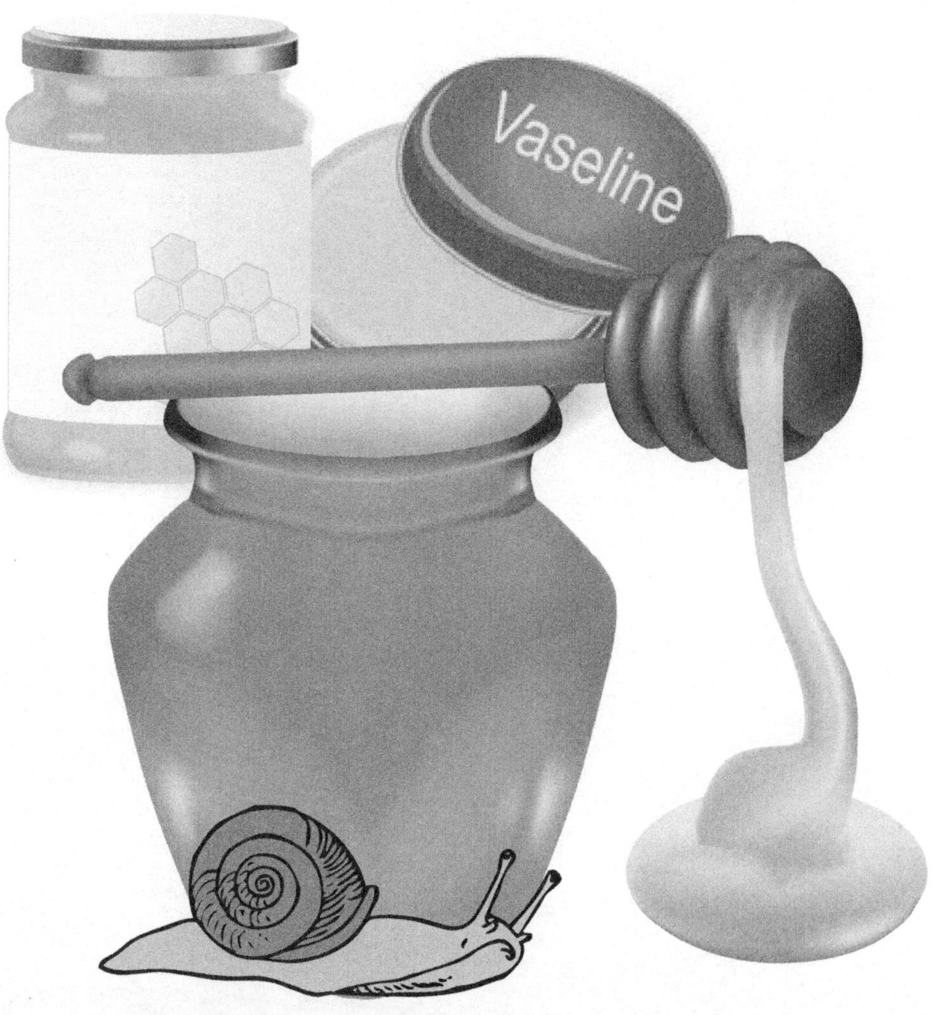

THIRD THING WE DO IS FIND A CLEAN OR DIRTY PLACE. YES, YOU READ IT RIGHT. IT ALL DEPENDS ON WHAT KIND OF A SLUG DO YOU WISH TO BE! A CLEAN ONE THAT LIVES IN THE HOUSE OR A DIRTY ONE THAT STRIVES IN YOUR BACKYARD

(DO THE DIRTY ONE IF YOU DO HAVE A BACKYARD, IF YOU DON'T, YOU CAN DO IT IN THE FOREST OR PUBLIC PARK ALONE AT NIGHT. IF YOU GET CAUGHT, DON'T EVER MENTION THIS BOOK OR ME).

EXTRA STEP, IT IS NOT NECESSARY, BUT YOU MIGHT CONSIDER A MAT OR A CARPET. IT WILL MAKE CLEANING EASIER, WHEN YOU ARE DONE PRETENDING TO BE A SLUG. UNLESS YOU WISH TO CONCEDE HUMANITY AND STAY A SLUG FOREVER. (WHICH IS A RESPECTFUL CHOICE OF A LIFESTYLE.)

ANOTHER EXRTA STEP IS A SERIOUS MATTER. YOU HAVE TO WEAR EYE-GOGGLES OR KEEP YOUR EYES CLOSED AND PROTECTED FOR THE MOST OF THE PROCEDURE. TRUST ME, IF HONEY OR VASELINE GETS INTO YOUR EYES, THE CONSEQUENCES WILL BE DAMAGING AND HURTFUL. HAVE A BOTTLE OR A BUCKET OF WATER NEAR YOU IN CASE YOU NEED TO CLEAN SOMETHING.

ALRIGHT!
NOW THAT YOU ARE PREPARED BOTH PHYSICALLY AND MENTALLY, WE CAN START.

POUR THE OOZE OF YOUR CHOOSING. START FROM HEAD AND LET IT SLOWLY DRIP DOWN ON YOUR SKIN TO YOUR TOES. YOU WILL SENSE AN AMAZING GOOEY FEELING AS TINY DRIPS OF STICKY MUSH TICKLE YOUR SENSITIVE AREAS.

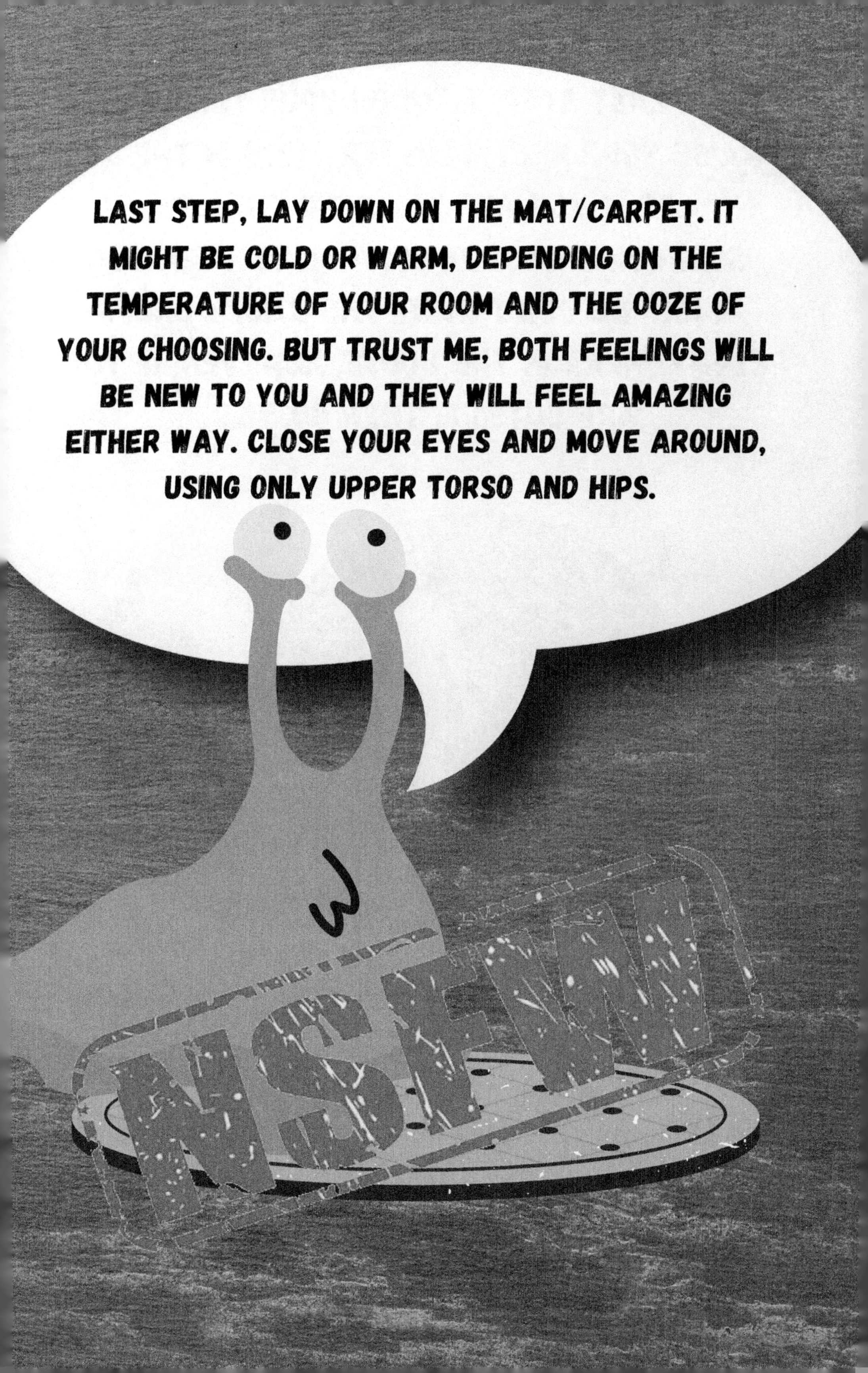
LAST STEP, LAY DOWN ON THE MAT/CARPET. IT MIGHT BE COLD OR WARM, DEPENDING ON THE TEMPERATURE OF YOUR ROOM AND THE OOZE OF YOUR CHOOSING. BUT TRUST ME, BOTH FEELINGS WILL BE NEW TO YOU AND THEY WILL FEEL AMAZING EITHER WAY. CLOSE YOUR EYES AND MOVE AROUND, USING ONLY UPPER TORSO AND HIPS.
NSFW

LAST, LAST STEP. TURN ON YOUR TUMMY AND RAISE YOUR FEET, FLUTTER THEM IN THE AIR AS IF YOU ARE ENJOYING THE NEW SURROUNDINGS. BUT DON'T MOVE THEM TOO MUCH, WE DON'T WANT THE STICKY DROPS EVERYWHERE IN THE HOUSE. HOWEVER, IF YOU ARE OUTSIDE, THEN GO WILD.

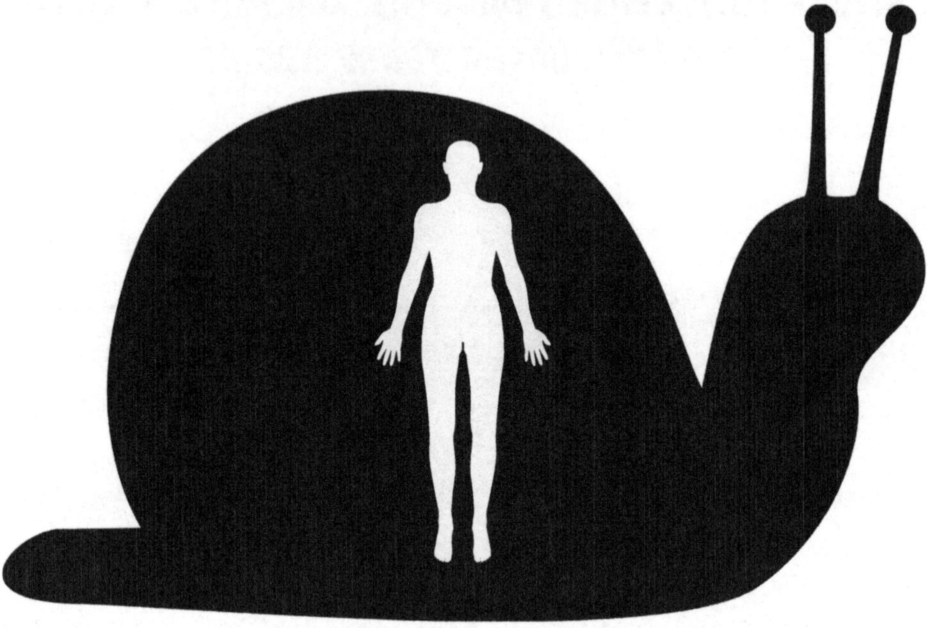

I AM KIDDING. DON'T GO WILD

Have you ever observed slugs and how slow they are, as if they don't care about time?
It is not because they are lazy or tired. It is because they have solved the meaning of life.

They are not in a hurry as we humans are. They do not plan weeks or even months ahead, stressing every single detail, pulling out hair and biting nails. The main problem that faces millions of Americans, as well as people all over the world is running out of time.

Now that you are a true slug , you have to change your life to fit their nature. How about I give you some of my life experienced rambling. You don't have to take any of my word as an advice or follow them. But this is something I wish I had someone tell me when I was younger.

The rambling starts, now.

"Youth needs guidance, not criticism"
Gandalf, probably

FINAL LAST STEP, NOW YOU CAN PROUDLY SAY
I AM
A
SLUG!
SAY IT AGAIN, BUT LOUDER. IF YOUR NEIGHBOR
CALLS THE MENTAL HOSPITAL ON YOU, THEN
YOU DID IT. YOU BECAME A SLUG

Time is something we humans have created and it is killing us without us knowing. No other animal checks the time. They do not know what time it is, what time it was and what time it will be. Slugs live today's life, rather than in the future or in the past. We should learn something from them.

Now I am not saying you shouldn't plan or remember the past, no, that is not my message. My message is for you not to stress out because of uncontrolled outcomes. What happened, What happens, and what will happen should not bring your anxiety to a point where it destroys your life.

Whether you plan it or not. Whether you want it or not. Accept the outcome as is and learn from it. Solve it or leave it. Move on.

I am old now. My mind is filled with ocean of regrets every time I close my eyes and go to bed. Does it sound like you? Well, you are not alone. Almost everyone that I know has this problem.

The solution is simple. You didn’t know better. You were younger than you are now, you have learned the lesson and improved yourself, and you will not do it again. And the biggest of all, you are the only person who remembers.

Forty-five years ago, I made fun of my physics teacher. When she wrote something on the board, I mimicked her and the class giggled. I did that multiple times until one time she caught me and I felt embarrassed.

Even today I still regret doing that to her. But when I asked my friends, they don't remember me ever doing that. Nobody remembers the regretful thing that you did. Nobody except for you.

You are literally killing yourself with those bad thoughts of regret. It will get worse if you don’t do anything about it. Trust me, it will.

Let go of the thoughts. Let go of regrets. They don't matter. The past is past, you cannot change it, but what you can change is the future. Be a better version of yourself and let those whom you wronged see, how amazing you are. And if they were the ones who wronged you, know this, they are human and make mistakes too, just as you do.

Take a deep breath and stay with me. Exhale slowly.... slower...even slower.

Take another deep breath. Feeling better?

Ask yourself, what is it that you always wanted?
Gaming? Cooking? Reading? Exercising?

Go and do it. Life is short. You don't have time to waste worrying about things you should have done. I'll say it again. Go and do it.

Now let's talk about another problem most people face in today's world. Ever heard of the phrase,

Money is the root of all evil?

Well actually it is false.

The root of all evil is greed or love for money, and not the money itself.
Money is just a currency that allows you to trade things.

Nothing less, nothing more.

Slugs do not worry about having big bank and lots of money. They are content with what they have, and so should all of us.

"Well of course, Ben." You will say. "Slugs have it good. All they do is eat, shit and sleep. They do not need to pay rent, groceries, mobile, internet, insurance, gas and etc."

Yes, I agree. However, that is not what I am saying.
Money is important. Actually, it is very important. It brings you a sense of security. You do not lose sleep if you can't come up with a bill payment. Trust me, I get it. I was there, collecting cents just to make it through the month.

What helped me wasn't investing. I didn't have money to invest. I had rent to pay and groceries to buy.

Not changing jobs, because I didn't have a fancy degree nor a skilled experience.
Not hustling, I wasn't bright and didn't know where and how to start a business.
And not stealing. I was never a criminal, no matter how hard it was for me.

What I did was,
I stopped using my credit card and had a financial budget plan.

I started to live a life of a minimalist. I bought things that I needed and nothing more. I didn't go eat out in a fancy restaurant. I didn't have an expensive phone or a data plan. I didn't even have a car until I was 38

I stuck to my plan and
I got out of debt at the age of 44.

at 49, I finally saved enough and bought a house with a lovely lady.

At 55, I opened my own retail store.

At 60, I speak to young kids in high school about life.

Even though back at 35, I was broke, depressed, and lonely.
I didn't know what to do with my life.

Life is a journey. It is a marathon. Keep going and it will surprise you.

First step of becoming content is accept who you are. Slugs do it and so can you. Let's test a few possibilities and answer this simple question.

Do you always compare yourself to those who are more successful?

It is as if they have figured life!

They are independent

They are free to do what they want

They have followers on Instagram and twitter

They are lying to you.

I have a friend who owns a big house, a beautiful white BMW and thousands of followers on his social media accounts!

Well, to tell you the truth.

He hates his life.

He had to save a lot of money and not spend a single dime on himself, just to save for down payment. The car that everyone gazes as he drives by, costs him an arm and a leg each month in insurance and gas prices. Followers on Instagram? I don't know about you, but he had received death threats from random people that he never met. And somehow, they knew where he lived, where he worked and names of his loved ones.

He had suffered extreme anxiety and fear when he received a picture from unknown number of a guy wearing a mask, standing next to his sleeping posture in his own bed, in his own house. He had to send his wife and kids to in-laws upstate.

Does that sound like a happy life for you? Well it didn't seem so for me.

Sure, money brings many joys of life, but it comes at a cost.

Try to live your life as best as you can. I know it is easier to preach, but I went through it.
You are a strong person. You can do it too. I know you can.

Now about friends and relatives. Ha-ha. If you truly love your relatives, here is the best advice. Don't ever get rich. Because if you do, be prepared to lose them. They will be asking you for your hard-earned money. It is a fact. Once you refuse, guess what? They are gone from your life. But if it is fine with you, then there is no true loss. They only wanted you for your money anyway.

So, you were born ugly, hairless, and short. Have you ever seen Slugs? They are the ugliest creatures on the planet, and yet they exist. They have a purpose and so do you.

People called you horrid names, because of the way you look and it bothers you to a point where you cannot think of anything else, but how to look like a TV actor or the models on the front cover of a beauty magazine.

Oh, my sweet child. Once I hit sixty-something, looks no longer mattered anymore.

Nobody will care if you looked like a Greek god in your twenties.

But do you know what they do remember?
The things that I have done.

I volunteered at the local food-shelter, and the people who often attended the place, remember me today. I wrote books. I taught students philosophy. I planted trees, with my city's community and people remember what we did, every time we take a shade under a tree from the blazing sun.

I take pride of the good things I have done and so should you. People measure you by the size of your heart, not by the size of your flippers. Remember, action speaks louder than words. Show them that you are a beautiful person with your actions and don't let them take you down with just words.

You are not obese, but that stomach fat is not going away. You are the shortest man among your friends that girls don't even see you. Yes, yes and yes. I've been in all of those categories.

What I did next surprised me the most. I started dieting. I quit sugar, soft drinks, cakes, bread and fries. I ate salad, fruit, meat, rice and drank lots and lots of water. Believe me or not, but I lost so much weight in one month that it motivated me to keep going. Half a year later, I started exercising, jogging, lifting weights, swimming, hiking and biking. These things do not need gym and are very cheap. So, there is no excuse not to do them. I lost over thirty pounds and felt great. I gained confidence and was not shy to take my shirt off on the beach.

You can't make yourself taller, but you can make yourself interesting. Learn new things every day, and impress a girl (or a boy) with your knowledge as intelligence is the most attractive attribute in a person. But if they still don't find you charming because you are short, you don't need those kind of people in your life, trust me.

You are never too old to start, so start now. Don't start tomorrow, because tomorrow will never come.

If anything, I want you to take this from me. Balance your life with entertainment and productivity. I understand how many of us can spent hours playing video games, watching a show on Netflix or anime on Crunchyroll. Stay away from Instagram, twitter, TikTok and Facebook and get closer to the Books.

Balance it and be productive.

Go for a walk. Do ten-pushups. Read a book. Clean your room. Mown the grass, plant a tree, wash your car. Cook a meal, eat a fruit, drink a glass of water.

Learn a language, listen to music, call a friend. Play a chess game, watch a documentary, and last but not least, meditate.

You will lose. You will win. Do not let the defeat turn you into a permanent loser, and do not let the win turn you into contemptible person.
Stay humble!

You are not a failure just because you do not know what to do with your life. Remember that.
You are a just child that hasn't explored yourself.

Samuel L. Jackson starred in his first movie when he was 46

Sam Walton opened the first Wal-Mart Store at 44

Charles Darwin published his first book 'The Origin of Species' at 50

Stan Lee created his first comic at the age of 39

Go slow and steady. You'll find yourself. When you do, you will feel as if life is giving you a second chance. Do not let it slip by.

You are* Beautiful! *No matter what people say, Beauty is in the heart. It is in your soul. It is in your smile.

Smile plenty.
It is the greatest weapon against the heaters.

And you know that you have matured when you realize that everyone's actions, behavior and body language is a mirror of what's going on inside of them.

Learn to read them. Analyze them. And try to stay away from those who dance with fake shoes.

You may never achieve your goal and die trying to get it. But you will die knowing that you did your best, rather than feeling an empty heart that hasn't even began to try, regretting day and night for that chance that has already gone by.

In the end, we will all end up in the grave. So live your life to the fullest, and do not worry about the future or past. Anything can happen.

You made it to the end I am proud of you, you little

SLUG

The End

Printed in Great Britain
by Amazon

84481718R10032